Summary
of

Behold the Dreamers
Imbolo Mbue

Conversation Starters

By BookHabits

Please Note: This is an unofficial conversation starters guide. If you have not yet read the original work, please do so first. Buy the book here.

We hope you enjoy this complementary guide from BookHabits. Our mission is to aid readers and reading groups with quality, thought provoking material to in the discovery and discussions on some of today's favorite books.

Tips for Using BookHabits Conversation Starters:

EVERY GOOD BOOK CONTAINS A WORLD FAR DEEPER THAN the surface of its pages. The characters and their world come alive through the words on the pages, yet the characters and its world still live on. Questions herein are designed to bring us beneath the surface of the page and invite us into the world that lives on. These questions can be used to:

- Foster a deeper understanding of the book
- Promote an atmosphere of discussion for groups
- Assist in the study of the book, either individually or corporately
- Explore unseen realms of the book as never seen before

About Us:

THROUGH YEARS OF EXPERIENCE AND FIELD EXPERTISE, from newspaper featured book clubs to local library chapters, *BookHabits* can bring your book discussion to life. Host your book party as we discuss some of today's most widely read books.

Table of Contents

Introducing *Behold The Dreamers*

*B*EHOLD THE DREAMERS IS THE CRITICALLY-ACCLAIMED debut novel by Imbolo Mbue which tells the story of how two couples--one immigrant, the other American-- strive for the good life but the economy collapses and both couples go through dramatic consequences. Set during the financial crash in 2008, Mbue's fast-paced, character-driven narrative impressed critics for its well-crafted plot and timely theme. It comes at a time when America is going through unrest and division as it tackles the controversial issue of immigration. The novel won the 2017 PEN/Faulkner Award for Fiction, named One of the Notable Books of 2017 by *The New York Times* and *The Washington Post,* and was selected by Oprah Winfrey for her 2017 Oprah's Book Club picks.

+ pg. 6

Jende and Neni Jonga emigrated from Cameroon and are working hard to achieve their dreams in America. After being employed as chauffeur by Lehman Brothers executive Carl Edwards, Jende now finds his dreams getting closer to reality. He had arrived in the US on a visitor's visa, and had been hoping to transform this to a green card. He had been working as a taxi driver in New York and had been able to bring over his wife Neni and son Liomi to America after two years' toil. Neni is now studying to become a pharmacist, having arrived with a student visa. Though living in a roach-ridden apartment in Harlem, the Jongas are hopeful. They are seeing their American Dream slowly getting real, thanks to their wealthy employer Clark Edwards. His wife Cindy and their two sons have slowly taken to the Jongas, as Cindy and Neni and the two couples' sons get to know each other better. The Jongas get an intimate view of the life of the Edwards and what appears to be the ultimate American dream that immigrants aspire for-- a big house, parties and vacations, and all the luxuries that wealth entails. They also see the unsavory side to it – the secrets and lying, marriage problems, and children going astray. When the financial crash happens and Lehman Brothers is among those implicated, the American Dream is suddenly threatened. Life for the two families turn ugly as they face the fearsome consequences of losing their jobs, and for the Edwards, their properties. Characters reveal their worst sides, conflict escalates, and friendships and marriages are threatened.

Mbue depicts two sides of the American Dream through the lives of the Edwards and the Jongas. Though the dream is achievable and America promises great reward to those who work hard, this doesn't always work for all immigrants who have to follow rules set by the often confusing immigration system. While we see the Edwards as the full example of dreams achieved to the fullest, we also see in them how dreams can fail. As immigrants, the Jongas experience the failure of dreams in the most heart-rending way. A question that arises is -- up to what extent can dreamers hold on to their dreams if reality makes them almost impossible to achieve. Being an immigrant herself, Mbue ably presents the stories of Cameroonian immigrants who dream big. The sad picture of how dreams are dashed to pieces is presented and the immigration question that is much debated among Americans loom big. What Mbue aspires to do is to give readers a closer look at the lives involved without moralizing.

The well-drawn characters enchant readers with their inner conflicts and aspirations, particularly in the women in the novel. Cindy is a generous employer but is also self-centered and secretive. Neni is exuberant, hopeful yet entirely complex. According to a review, the men in the novel seem to take the effects of the financial upheaval in less dramatic ways than the women. Yet all four characters act and drive the plot to its end.

Another main theme is the class divide that is so obvious in the contrasting lifestyles of the Edwards and the Jongas. The author paints the good life enjoyed by the Edwards in their luxurious surroundings while the Jongas try to make do with their dark, insect-infested hovel. The theme of cultural encounters and misunderstandings is likewise highlighted in the relations between the two couples. The immigrant experience seen from the eyes of the Jongas is a revealing one: Neni experiences a change of identity as she blends into the American ways, while Jende is puzzled with the excesses apparent in the food culture elevated into artistic experience by the Americans. The idea of home arises among the immigrants as they think back of what their life used to be, and how they hope to establish a better home in America. Leaving one's home of birth to find a better home abroad is a theme that makes the immigrant experience emotionally complex.

Rich in themes that are relevant and touching, Mbue's novel is called by Book Reporter review as "unique, poignant and striking". Apart from winning major awards, the novel was also the Best Book of 2016 by The Guardian, NPR, Kirkus Reviews, Amazon, the San Francisco Chronicle, and The St. Louis Dispatch. The novel likewise won the 2017 Blue Metropolis Words to Change Award.

Introducing the Author

IMBOLO MBUE LEFT HER HOMETOWN OF LIMBE IN CAMEROON for the United States in 1998. She became a citizen after 16 years, in 2014. She took her BS degree in Rutgers University, and her MA in Columbia University. She currently lives in New York City.

Becoming a 2017 Oprah's Book Club selection is one of the highlights of Mbue's writing career and also a fulfillment of her own American Dream. She was in fact inspired to become a writer through Oprah's Book Club. When she was younger and not yet a writer, she visited a library in Falls Church, Va. where she saw a shelf dedicated to Oprah's Book Club selections. She picked Toni Morrison's *Song of Solomon* which amazed and inspired her. Today, she remains a fan of the club, reading selections like *The Poisonwood Bible* by Barbara Kingsolver and

Middlsex by Jeffrey Euginedes. She was ecstatic when she was informed by Oprah herself that her *Behold The Dreamers* is chosen as 2017 Oprah Book Club pick.

The idea of the American Dream had always been present in Mbue's consciousness, as early as when she was a young girl still living in Limbe, Cameroon. Being a seaside town visited by Western tourists for its black sand beaches, she saw how Cameroonians aspired to the prosperous life that the American tourists had. The locals saw how America made her countrymen's dreams come true through material wealth, homes and luxuries achieved by those who went to America. Mbue of course knows how such dreams are not as sweet as they seem to be and her debut novel is proof of this.

In an interview with Jeffrey Brown of PBS, Mbue reveals her thoughts about the immigration issue that is passionately debated in the US today. Being an immigrant herself, she has much empathy for her Cameroonian characters, but she also extended effort to know more about her American couple, the Edwards, who also struggle hard to maintain the American Dream they are living. Both her Cameroonian and American couples have their own struggles, and with the collapse of the economy, they had to deal with the consequences.

Unlike the Jongas who had to go back home to Cameroon, Mbue is able to establish a successful career in America. She inked a million-dollar deal in 2014, allowing *Behold the Dreamers* to be published by Random House. She is aware of her situation—an immigrant and a citizen at the same time. Having made clear the plight of immigrants who have a hard time establishing themselves in the country, she also knows that she has a responsibility as a citizen "to think about America's future."

Mbue was unemployed when she started writing the book. She lost her job as a result of the 2008 financial crisis. She saw that a lot of immigrants were employed as chauffeurs during that time, seeing them park their luxury cars in front of the Time Warner Center. She wondered how they fared during the crisis and that was how the novel came into being.

Mbue continues to show interest in her country of origin. She recently became concerned of the unrest in Cameroon when the Anglophone population protested against discrimination by the predominantly francophone government. Mbue herself is an Anglophone and therefore belongs to this linguistic minority in Cameroon. She witnessed how Anglophones like her were treated as second-class citizens in her own country. When she came to the US for college, she realized, to her delight, that everybody is Anglophone. She was not anymore discriminated against because of her language. Ironically, she continued to feel the stress of being a second-class citizen, this time, because of her status as an immigrant.

Discussion Questions

"Get Ready to Enter a New World"

Tip: Begin with questions dealing with broader issues to ensure ample time for quality discussions. Read through all discussion questions before engaging.

~ ~ ~

question 1

A main theme in the novel is chasing the American Dream. By moving to America, immigrants believe that they can have a brighter future for their families. Jende Jonga and his wife were full of hopes as they inched closer to fulfilling their dreams when Jende got the job as a chauffeur. Do you think the author presented the theme convincingly through her characters? Were you able to have a deeper understanding of what motivates immigrants to come to the US?

~ ~ ~

~ ~ ~

question 2

The two couples in the story occupy opposite positions in the social ladder. While Clark Edwards and his wife Cindy belong to the top 1 percent wealthy, Jende Jonga and wife Nenia are way down below, among the poorest in America. Despite the difference, do the two couples share the same hopes for their children? How different are they when it comes to parenting styles? How similar?

~ ~ ~

~ ~ ~

question 3

As chauffeur to the Edwards family, Jende witnesses the kind of family relations, conflicts, misunderstandings and pressures on the family. How does he interpret and react to what he witnesses? How does this influence his belief on the American dream?

~ ~ ~

~~~

question 4

The contrast in social position between Clark and Jende is immediately highlighted in the novel's first chapter. While Clark is a self-confident top executive Jende looks shabby and full of doubts as an immigrant seeking employment. What are the ways that their social standing affect their personalities and ways of thinking?

~~~

~~~

question 5

The contrast between their wives Cindy and Neni is also shown in many ways. Cindy as the privileged wife is generous and kind but not socially aware and often self-centered while Neni is hard-working and hopeful but not without fault too. They however share the same concerns as women and wives trying to do the proper thing for their families. How are they similar? What bonds them as women, wives and mothers?

~~~

~ ~ ~

question 6

As immigrants, Jende and Neni bring with them their identities and cultural traits as Cameroonians. As they adjust to the American environment, they find themselves slowly accommodating American ways, starting with their speaking and expressing themselves in English. How else do they change as the novel progresses? Are these good or bad? Why?

~ ~ ~

~ ~ ~

question 7

The narrative is driven by the collapse of the American economy and the repercussions on the Edwards family and on their chauffeur Jende and his family. The two couples' relationship struggles also contribute to the direction of the story. In what way do their relationships drive the story's events?

~ ~ ~

~ ~ ~

question 8

As immigrants, Jende and Neni have a unique perspective into American culture. They can see American ways and lifestyle from a point totally different from the privileged, wealthy, modern, and fast-paced. What are the observations made by them that you find striking? Why?

~ ~ ~

~ ~ ~

question 9

Though far from their land of birth, Jende and Neni still
remember Cameroon dearly. Though they love their country,
they also have criticisms against the way it is run by its leaders.
Why do you think they are still strongly attached to their home
country despite leaving it for America? What are your thoughts
about the conflicting sentiments about loving one's home
country even if one decides to live in another?

~ ~ ~

question 10

Eventually, Jende and Neni had to back back home to Cameroon. Their stay in the US has become impossible due to the economic crash and immigration laws. How did you feel about reading this part in the novel? What does this say of the myth of the American dream?

~ ~ ~

~~~

question 11

As their employers, Clark and Cindy Edwards dictate the terms of how they want Jende and Neni to serve them. A requirement is for Jende to keep private everything that he hears and sees in the Edwards home. Do you think the Edwards are fair in their dealings with the Jongas? Do the Jongas stay within the expectations as employees or do they become more than employees at times? What is the real nature of the two couples' relations with each other?

~~~

~ ~ ~

question 12

The Edwards son Vince decides to leave his law studies and go to India for some soul-searching. This is an American privilege among those who can afford to travel and who have the option to forego or delay college education. How important are his thoughts and ideas about his country in the narrative? How does he figure in the immigrants' pursuit of the American dream?

~ ~ ~

~~~

question 13

Carl Edwards is a top executive at Lehman brothers. As an executive and family man he has many sides to him. What part does he play in the collapse of the company? Do you think he is a good person? Why? Why not?

~~~

~~~

question 14

The characters' pursuit of dreams move the story forward in the novel. Jende and Neni have dreams that they want to achieve. They're willing to work hard for these dreams. When the dreams start to become seemingly impossible, they had to confront the reality and conflicts arise. Is the dream theme an effective devise for the narrative? Why?

~~~

~ ~ ~

question 15

The Jongas had no options left and had to give up their dreams
and go back home. They realized that their dream of a better life
is not possible as they thought, and is much complicated by
immigration laws and regulations. What can you say about the
immigration system in America? Is it too strict for immigrants or
fair for everybody? Why?

~ ~ ~

~ ~ ~

question 16

Book Reporter review says *Behold the Dreamers* has characters that are "superbly wrought and believable". The author depicted authentic characters who are neither entirely good nor bad, but people who are trying to improve their conditions in life. Do you agree with the reviewer? Can you explain how the characters are neither good nor bad?

~ ~ ~

~~~

question 17

This is a debut novel by Imbolo Mbue. It won the 2017 PEN/Faulkner Award for Fiction and cited one of the Notable Books of 2016 by *The New York Times* and *The Washington Post*. Why do you think it is a critically acclaimed book? What literary factors contributed to the book's success?

~~~

~ ~ ~

question 18

The novel is Oprah Winfrey's book club latest selection, as of June 2017. Winfrey has chosen other debut novels in the past. Being chosen by Winfrey has helped many books become bestsellers and achieve book awards. Do you think Mbue's novel will achieve bestseller status?

~ ~ ~

~~~

question 19

The Boston Globe review says Mbue has "narrative energy and sympathetic eye" which made the story an irresistible read. Can you cite the narrative energy in the novel? How are the characters drawn with a sympathetic eye?

~~~

~ ~ ~

question 20

The Seattle Times review says the novel is about the meeting of two cultures that end up not having "an accurate angle on each other". How do you understand this statement? Do you agree with it?

~ ~ ~

~~~

question 21

Imbolo Mbue arrived in the US in 1998 and became a citizen in 2014. She first started writing the novel with the financial crisis as the main theme. Eventually, the novel became a story about immigration as well. Why do you think the writing of the novel eventually included the immigration theme? Do you think the American financial crisis' impact on immigrants was unavoidable?

~~~

~ ~ ~

question 22

When she was growing up in Cameroon, Mbue saw how the American dream took hold among her people. They thought of America as a promised land where wealth and success is achievable. With her novel's critical acclaim and selected by Oprah Winfrey for her book club, do you think she herself is an example of the American dream come true? Compare her success to that of the characters in her book.

~ ~ ~

~ ~ ~

question 23

Immigration is currently a controversial issue in the US. Mbue's novel explored this topic in her novel by telling the story of Cameroonian immigrants. What do you think is Mbue's stand on the issue? Do you agree with her?

~ ~ ~

~ ~ ~

question 24

The *New York Time* review describes the novel as "capacious, big-hearted." It says the way Neni described America applies likewise to the novel itself – "a magnificent land of uninhibited dreamers." Can you say that Mbue is also an uninhibited dreamer? Is her book's success proof of this?

~ ~ ~

~~~

question 25

A reviewer highlighted Mbue's sympathetic eye in depicting her characters. She admitted in an interview that her sympathy was clearly for the Jongas because she herself is an immigrant. Do you think Mbue was able to portray the Edwards with a sympathetic eye as well? Can you cite instances where she did this?

~~~

~ ~ ~

question 26

Mbue started writing the novel when she was unemployed. She was one of the casualties of the financial crisis. If she did not experience unemployment do you think she would have written a novel like this? Would she have written a different kind of debut novel instead?

~ ~ ~

~~~

question 27

The story happened during the 2008 financial crisis in the US. If the Jongas arrived in the US on the years not affected by the crisis, how do you think the narrative would change? Would being employed by the Edwards result to a different outcome? Would immigration be an issue?

~~~

~ ~ ~

question 28

In the end, the Jongas had to return to Cameroon because their dreams and plans in America did not work out despite their hard work. If Mbue changed her ending to a happier one, do you think it would be believable? Why? Why not?

~ ~ ~

~ ~ ~

question 29

The Jongas were from Cameroon, the same country where Mbue
is from. If the novel was written by an Asian or Eastern European,
do you think it would have been equally interesting and
successful? Are you aware of any American Dream stories by
other immigrants? How similar and different are they to Mbue's
novel?

~ ~ ~

~ ~ ~

question 30

The contrast between the wealthy Edwards and the poor Jongas highlighted the issue of class divide in America. If Mbue used characters who are not too rich and not too poor, do you think the story would be equally interesting? Why? Why not?

~ ~ ~

~ ~ ~

question 31

Mbue lost her job as staff of a media marketing department during the financial crash and wondered how the drivers for executives who worked at the Time Warner Center in Manhattan were affected as well. She initially intended to write a novel about the financial crisis but eventually expanded the theme to include immigration and the American Dream.

~ ~ ~

~ ~ ~

question 32

Behold the Dreamers presents two sides of the American Dream by putting together the issues of financial crisis and immigration. The characters of Jende and Neni have a view of the wonderful promise of a better life in America but also the economic difficulties that affect America's immigrants.

~ ~ ~

~~~

question 33

As an immigrant herself, Mbue knows the lives of people like Jende and Neni but knows very little about the top one percent wealthy like the Edwards. She had to exert more effort to know the lives of the privileged, their struggles and the demands to maintain a life that the majority of people dream of.

~~~

~ ~ ~

question 34

Mbue admits that she was much like Jende and Neni when she came to America. She saw the country as the Promised Land. She still believes that the US has a lot to offer to immigrants but the American Dream is not accessible to everybody.

~ ~ ~

~~~

question 35

Mbue says that the novel does not tell people what to think about immigration. As an author, her task is to tell stories honestly and completely, so that people of different cultures will understand each other.

~~~

~~~

question 36

Before she became a writer, Mbue once went to a library in Falls Church, Va., and saw a shelf full of Oprah book club picks. She chose Toni Morrison's *Song of Solomon* which inspired her to write.

~~~

~ ~ ~

question 37

Oprah Winfrey's OWN network and *O Magazine* announced to the *Associated Press* that Mbue's *Behold the Dreamers* is the latest selection for Oprah's book club. Winfrey said the novel was topical and timeless. Mbue had always been a fan of Winfrey's book club and was ecstatic when Winfrey told her in a phone call that *Dreamers* was her latest pick.

~ ~ ~

~ ~ ~

question 38

The Boston Globe review cites the dishonesty apparent in the characters and the political and economic systems that force the characters into such dishonesty. Lies between the characters are repeated in the lies that Lehman Brothers does to people, including lies to immigrants who buy their dream homes. The novel is critical in this instance, but it is also hopeful.

~ ~ ~

~~~

question 39

Presidents Barack Obama and Donald Trump appear in the novel. Jende and Neni were ecstatic when Obama won the elections, raising their hopes that they are nearer to accomplishing their dreams. They planned to go to a restaurant at the Trump Hotel to celebrate once Neni finishes her studies; Trump will cook steak for them.

~~~

~ ~ ~

question 40

The Jonga couple come from the town of Limbe in Cameroon. This is the hometown of Mbue. It is a seaside city popular among Western tourists for its black sand beaches. The constant contact with tourists has made the American Dream an aspiration among the locals.

~ ~ ~

Quiz Questions

"Ready to Announce the Winners?"

Tip: Create a leaderboard and track scores to see who gets the most correct answers. Winners required. Prizes optional.

~ ~ ~

quiz question 1

Chasing the _____ is a main theme in *Behold the Dreamers*. Immigrants believe that they can have a brighter future if they work hard enough in America. Mbue shows in her novel the two sides to this aspiration.

~ ~ ~

~ ~ ~

quiz question 2

Jende is employed as _____ for Clark Edwards and his family. His job allows him to witness the private details of the Edwards family and a view of the American way of life.

~ ~ ~

~ ~ ~

quiz question 3

True or False: Clark Edwards works as an executive for Time Warner Bros. He enjoys a high salary that allows his family to live in luxury.

~ ~ ~

~~~

quiz question 4

True or False: Jende was confident and well-dressed for the interview with Clark Edwards. He knew exactly what to say if questioned about his immigration status because he is fully honest about it.

~~~

~ ~ ~

quiz question 5

Neni arrived in the US with a _____ visa. She is hopeful that with her education, she will be able to land a job that will earn her much money.

~ ~ ~

~~~

quiz question 6

True or False: The Jonga family are from Cameroon. They continue to love their country of origin despite their decision to leave and have a new life in America.

~~~

~ ~ ~

quiz question 7

_____ Edwards decided to forego his law studies and travel to India instead. He has his own ideas about America which contribute to an understanding of the American Dream.

~ ~ ~

~ ~ ~

quiz question 8

Mbue arrived in the US in 1998 and became a citizen in the year
_____. Losing her job during the financial crisis, she wondered
how other immigrants were affected as well. This was how the
book came about.

~ ~ ~

~ ~ ~

quiz question 9

True or False: When she was growing up, Mbue saw how the American Dream took hold among fellow Cameroonians. They believed that America is a land of promise where dreams of wealth and a better life are achievable.

~ ~ ~

~ ~ ~

quiz question 10

Mbue is an _____ and belonged to the linguistic minority in Cameroon. When she came to the US, she was glad that her language did not make her a minority and a second-class citizen.

~ ~ ~

~~~

quiz question 11

Mbue's Behold the Dreamers won the _____ . The award makes her book critically acclaimed and establishes her as an award-winning author.

~~~

~~~

quiz question 12

True or False: Mbue's novel was selected as part of the Oprah's Book Club picks for 2017. The author was ecstatic about the recognition because Oprah's Book Club inspired her to become a writer.

~~~

Quiz Answers

1. American Dream
2. Chauffeur
3. False
4. False
5. Student
6. True
7. Vince
8. 2014
9. True
10. Anglophone
11. 2017 PEN/Faulkner Award for Fiction
12. True

Ways to Continue Your Reading

EVERY month, our team runs through a wide selection of books to pick the best titles for readers and reading groups, and promotes these titles to our thousands of readers – sometimes with free downloads, sale dates, and additional brochures.

Want to register yourself or a book group? It's free and takes 1-click.

Register here.

On the Next Page...

Please write us your reviews! Any length would be fine but we'd appreciate hearing you more! We'd be SO grateful.

Till next time,

BookHabits

"Loving Books is Actually a Habit"

Made in the USA
Columbia, SC
02 February 2018